A LOST CHILDHOOD FROZEN IN TIME

ANDREW McDOWELL

Copyright © Andrew McDowell

For legal reasons, my name has been changed and only the first names of other people – staff and children – are used.
I have met some famous people in my life, and I have mentioned some names where possible, however, again for legal reasons, I cannot name all the well known people I have met.

Dedication

For my beautiful daughters Laura and Cloe.
For my brothers and sisters Christopher, Martin,
Ian, Jenny, Patsy, Wendy, Caroline and Christine.

So where does the journey come from?
To see it to its end.
It comes from within.
No matter how hard life hits.
You get up and keep moving forward.
Never give up.
As a survivor.
I will keep fighting.
No matter what.

Andrew McDowell

Acknowledgements

I have a very few close friends, but I would like to thank Ann-Marie and Tina, who were both a big inspiration, for me writing this book - especially Tina, who is such an amazing friend.

A massive thanks to Kenny and Jim, two loyal friends since school days, Kenny's family have all been brilliant. (I will never forget Kenny nicking my pencil at school - because of that, I got the belt).

Many thanks to Alex, my daughters godfather, you're a star.

Many thanks to my lovely friend in Scotland, Linda, your wise advice has always helped.

Thanks to Caroline and Neil (the mum and dad to my daughter's best friend Molly) who have been there for us in many ways.

My great friends, Phil, Gary, Jackie and Colin. Trish, Betty and Donny, his lovely daughter Julie. Rebecca for our lovely lunch meets. Jill - a beautiful woman inside and out - for those lovely chats. Special thanks to my lovely neighbours, Keith, Rachel, Becks.

I also can't thank Rachel from Future Pathways enough - your support has been amazing. Many thanks to Charlie Lea, of Read Now Write Now, and also to Mary at The Book Whisperers, both your support and knowledge about writing has been just fantastic.

This is my story of a lost childhood.

Contents Page

Foreword i

Introduction iii

Life Before Care 1

Coalgate Avenue, Tranent 3

Harmany School, Balerno 14

Back to Tranent 25

The Army 30

After the Army 37

Breaking the Ice 43

Foreword

By Mary Turner Thomson

In this memoir, Andrew McDowell courageously shares his painful journey through family abuse, trauma, and the devastating impact of a childhood in care. As the reader will learn, Andrew's story is one of resilience and hope, but it is also a story that sheds light on a dark reality that many children growing up in care have experienced.

Andrew's experience of being beaten by his mother, taken into care, and then subjected to further abuse is a story that is sadly all too common. The care system in the 1970s failed many vulnerable children, including Andrew, and the effects of that failure are still being felt today.

As you read Andrew's story, you will be struck by his honesty, courage, and unwavering determination to overcome the many challenges he has faced. Despite being separated from his siblings and left alone and isolated, Andrew found a way to break the ice and find a path forward. His story is a testament to the resilience of the human spirit and the power of hope.

At the heart of Andrew's story is a message that needs to be heard: the impact of childhood trauma can be devastating and far-reaching, affecting not just the person who experienced it but also their loved ones. Andrew's memoir is an important reminder that we must do more to support survivors of childhood abuse and ensure that no child has to go through what he did.

This is a powerful and inspiring book that will leave a lasting impression on the reader. Andrew's story is one that needs to be told, and I am honoured to have been asked to write the foreword for this memoir. I hope that this book will inspire others to find the strength and courage to speak their truth and heal from their own traumas.

Introduction

"Where are you?" Mum barked down the phone.
"I'm in Glasgow," I replied calmly.
"Aren't you coming home for leave?" she persisted.
"No, I'm not," I said firmly.
"Why not? This is your home!"
I took a deep breath before responding. "No, it's not my home and you're not my mother," I said feeling the weight of the past in my words. With that I slammed down the phone – the memories of my childhood trauma flooding back.

It had been years, but the wounds from being kicked out of my childhood home at five, the physical, mental, and sexual abuse in the care homes, and my attempts to take my own life still hadn't fully healed. So when my biological mother tried to claim me, and her home as mine, I couldn't help but push back.

I didn't feel that home was mine, nor that she deserved the title of my mum.

I still don't.

.oOo.

Being brought up in the care system in the 1970s was horrific, I was placed in several homes between 1970 and 1981 and I certainly wasn't the only child who suffered abuse, far from it.

The treatment I had in these various homes was very wrong and I've suffered both physical and indecent assaults which still, to this day, has an effect on me mentally and emotionally.

The Scottish Child Abuse Inquiry was set up in 2015 to look into cases of child abuse in care. In particular, they are looking into what happened, why, what, and where abuse took place; the effects of the abuse upon children and their families; whether the organisations responsible for children in care failed in their duties; and what changes to the law, policies or procedures are needed.

I received my social service records from Birth Link Scotland with all the relevant names blanked out. There are over 100 pages of records, and I was told that reading them would be too stressful and bad for my mental health. Apart from speaking to a solicitor about them, I took their advice and have not read them myself.

This story is based on my own memories of my life. It is my true account of the time I spent in care and a story of a lost childhood.

I hated my childhood due to this and the lies from the care system in Scotland. I have brothers and sisters, eight in all, of whom I still don't know properly to this day.

I was told that I would never be split up from my brothers and sisters, yet my youngest sister and one of my brothers were adopted. Then I was placed in one home without the others.

Although I have met a few of my siblings, we don't know each other. I also have nieces and nephews who I don't know as well. It was hurtful and sad not knowing and left me feeling isolated and alone.

My childhood was frozen in time. I had to break the ice on my own. Joining the army saved me from a life of drugs and probably drinking. I have always felt that I am the one fighting. I am a survivor, I fight on.

.oOo.

There is a song by Emeli Sande 'Read All About It - part III' – and if you listen to the lyrics you will have an idea of my life.

So how did I break the ice?

As a soldier, I was proud to have served my Queen and country. I became a Physical Training Instructor and was lucky enough to work on the Krypton Factor assault course.

I've met the late Queen and Princess Anne on several occasions. In fact, I did a marathon in 1986 and got to present cheque for around £500 to Princess Anne for the Save the Children charity, who still remembered who I was a year later. Army life was hard but good, it taught me discipline, respect and gave me the education I never had growing up.

I have even managed to be a dancer on the Hitman and Her - a British television dance music programme. They were great times, meeting lots of famous people such as Kylie Minogue, Jason Donovan, Nick Kamen as well as Pete Waterman and Michaela Strachan. All because I used to help a friend with his discos years ago. (Andy, if you get to read this book, hope you are well.)

Music has always been a big escape for me, especially in my childhood from the Sex Pistols to ska, northern soul, mod and dance music. Especially Ska music, as I love Madness, having seen them over 20 times, and will again this year. Two very special occasions with my daughter Cloe - which we both loved. I also like, The Beat, Bad Manners, The Specials, and The Selecter — all of this music was a big help during my childhood. Nowadays, well what can I say about the brilliant, Death Of Guitar Pop - just amazing. Bringing back Ska in a big way - their music has really helped me in the last few years.

It was not all plain sailing though. I've had failed relationships and once I found myself homeless, ending up sleeping on a friend's couch. I was lucky enough to get help - from Ted and Joyce - but I really had to get sorted and find a home.

I met someone from the Royal British Legion, they were fantastic in helping me, and where I am today is because of them. I eventually started helping with their Poppy Appeal, and I am now the poppy appeal organiser for where I live.

In 2021, I thought of running an art competition with local schools, to raise money for the Royal British Legion's 100th year. It went brilliantly. One of the schools celebrated by putting some of the children's artwork, on the walls. I believe the murals are still there. Then I was told that the northwest's poppy launch was going to be filmed in the village where I live. This was one of the proudest days of my life and amazing to see a small idea grow into all this. So thank you Ruth, and Judith from the Legion.

We hold the art competition every year now, many thanks to the other Ruth and the armed forces community - Willo, Bill, Gary, Dave, Kev and Barry and everyone else. We all worked together, to support events, and hope we do for many years.

I was also team manager of the Men's team for Warrington Athletic Club. In the three seasons I was there we went from Division Three to Division One and we were awarded Sports Team of the Year. I even got to meet Lord Sebastian Coe. Also great times at Warrington Athletics Club, were I have championship medals for cross country, and road relays, both Merseyside and Cheshire. Warrington AC is a brilliant club, I was proud to be part of it.

I also befriended a man whose garden I tended – and we formed a bond. Ultimately, he became like a father to me.

I now have my own house, two beautiful daughters, one who is now in university - I'm so proud of her. My older daughter is doing really well too.

It was not easy to break the ice, but I eventually did. I often wonder what it would be like to sit with my brothers and sisters and just share family time. Something that was ripped away from us all. I'm very lucky to have such great friends, you know who you are, thanks for being there always.

.oOo.

To all survivors of child abuse, never give up. I am now having treatment for this, it is not easy, many thanks to Veterans in Mind, who first saw this about my childhood, and to Mandy from the Royal British Legion, who was the first to actually say I have PTSD.

The future is now a bit brighter. As a survivor I will never give up, although I did often think about suicide.

I suppose the best is yet to come. I will always be so proud of my two girls... Over and out...!

Life Before Care

I can only remember some parts of my early life. We lived in an old stone, grey coloured house on a farm in Little Pinkerton in East Lothian, Scotland. There was me, my mum, Nancy, Dad, John, sister Jenny, sister Wendy was just a baby. And brother Martin. My other sister Patsy was living in a handicap hospital, though it would not be a good few years before I met her. My other brother Ian was adopted at birth, I have never seen him.

My Mum and Dad would always be fighting, and Mum would beat me lots of times. She once even tied me to a radiator.

One of my aunties came to visit and thought I was brain damaged from the beatings I took, so why did this auntie not take me away? She was surprised I was still alive. I was around four years old when this was going on.

I also found out years later that our mother hit my little sister with a milk bottle over the head, my sister was only a baby at the time.

I can remember me and my brother feeding Scottish meat pies to the donkey on the farm –, they were meant for our tea, oops!

Me and my brother Martin did, even at this young age, tried to kill ourselves. The first time we drank weed killer, lucky the farmer saw us and took us to Hospital. Then we tried to hang ourselves from the first-floor landing using our bed sheets, my sister Jenny saw us and stopped us from doing this.

I was only four years old at the time.

I don't remember my Dad leaving. It was only years later I found out he had re-married and had more children who told me he was a good man.

Apparently, my mother was having problems, so we were taken into care and placed in a family group home in Tranent, East Lothian Scotland.

Coalgate Avenue, Tranent

The place I first went to was a 'family group' home at 67 Coalgate Avenue, Tranent, East Lothian which was run by East Lothian Council.

It was a big house with a black gate on the entrance and a large tree in the front garden. It had some sort of concrete path that led up to the front door.

When you went into the house, I remember there being a living room on the right and the stairs over on the left. The kitchen was at the back on the right and there was also a domestic bedroom opposite the living room. Upstairs, there were two bedrooms on the left and one large bedroom on the right. There was also the bathroom which was directly opposite the stairs.

There were about eight children in the home. The first bedroom on the left was for a brother and sister called Stuart and Heather. After they left, two people, Julie and Cheryl, took their room. The second bedroom on the left was for my sister Jenny. I shared a bedroom with my brother Martin and a boy called Alastair. The bedroom downstairs was where the staff would stay when they worked overnight.

The staff who I remember first were a Mr and Mrs N. They were in charge of the home. He was about fifty years of age, well built, with grey hair and a grey moustache. Mrs N was about the same age, with curly grey hair, and was of a slim build.

Everything at the home was very strict and regimented. You would be woken up and go for breakfast and I remember that Mr and Mrs N would always make us pray before every meal.

I cannot recall Mr N doing anything to me, but Mrs N would repeatedly hit me on the head and hands with a wooden handled clothes brush, with had black bristles. She would also punish me by making me sit on the stairs for hours on end for no reason at all and I also remember her tying me to my bed of a night to make me stay there. This happened almost every day and night. If we moved or spoke, we were hit on the head with the wooden hairbrush.

All of the children suffered this. It was not because we had done anything wrong, they were just cruel bastards.

The treatment I received from Mrs N was terrifying and horrible, she was a very cruel woman. Her husband was definitely aware of what was going on.

I used to have this brown bear teddy. He was called 'Big Brown Bear'. I couldn't go to sleep unless he was at the bottom of my bed. When I was crying after being hurt or abused, I use to say to him, "Please help me and protect me." Having nothing or nobody to turn too, it was like I was in another world with my Big Brown Bear.

I cried most nights, terrified, feeling lost and alone. Especially in the first few years of the family group home in Coalgate. As Mr and Mrs N, and Anna, were there.

Stuart and Heather got the same treatment as me.

I had a social worker called Larry and I remember he asked why I had a lump on my head. I told him I had just fallen but Jenny spoke up and told him the truth, that Mrs N had hit me with there with the clothes brush.

Shortly after this, Mr & Mrs N were moved from the house. I never knew what happened to them both, never got told. I often wonder why, or this is covered up, or is it on record somewhere?

I think this was maybe around 1972/1973.

They were replaced by Margaret who arrived with her husband, George. He worked for an insurance company and shouldn't have had anything to do with what went on in the care home.

George was in his forties, well built and around six foot tall and always clean shaven, with tidy, short dark hair. I also remember that he played bowls.

Margaret was about thirty-eight to forty five years of age. She was slim with long blonde hair to her shoulders, with a good skin complexion.

In terms of general discipline, if you did something wrong, like fighting, you were made to stand in a corner facing the wall and be called a dunce. Sometimes the staff would hit you as well.

At this time, I had a bedwetting problem, and this was behind some of the treatment I received from them.

On one occasion, when me and my brother Martin were out playing, we never came back when we were supposed to. So when did return, George took us to our bedroom, and we were both made to lie on the bed next to each other before he strapped us on our bare buttocks with a brown leather belt as a punishment. I would say that he hit us about half a dozen times. He had no right to do this to us, he wasn't even a member of staff.

This wasn't the only time he strapped me, there were other occasions too. Margaret knew this went on but did not do anything about it.

With regards to being strapped, I do not recall any lasting injury and did not receive any medical treatment as a direct result of what happened.

Due to my bedwetting, one member of staff, Anna, used to get me out of bed several times during the night when she was on duty and make me go to the toilet. Oh boy did I hate her. She would pull my pants down and make me stand over 'the toilet' – in those days, a stone-cold floor. She would sit on the bath and then run the cold tap, saying things like, "You're not going to wet the bed tonight, you're going to do the toilet."

If I did not pee, I would be hit on the back of my legs and the genital area. I was then dragged back to bed, made to get up again and she would then do the same thing again. She would get very impatient with me, and I would be crying. She would mock me, especially in front of other children. I found this painful and very distressing.

Anna would make threats for no reason at all. She would say, "That Andrew, he will get it!"

I also used to hate her washing my hair as she would use scalding water and pin me against the side with my arms behind my back. She would then dig her fingernails into my scalp whilst washing my hair, saying, "I'll show you."

I got the impression she took pleasure out of doing this and I believe she was a very cruel woman.

My social worker, Larry, was alright. After what had happened with Mr and Mrs N, he told me if anything else happened then I was to tell him. The thing was, I was too scared of what would have happened to me if I spoke up, and so I never said anything to him.

.oOo.

At this time there was another incident that I experienced although it had nothing to do with the staff. I was out one day, near to the home by some playing fields close to the school. I remember I was out catching bees in a jar when I saw a man walking along the road.

He said to me, "What you doing there son?"

He was about forty to fifty years of age, slim build, with short very dark hair which was brushed back possibly with Brylcreem or something on it. I remember he was wearing a purple jacket and black trousers, and I remember his breath smelt strongly of alcohol. He also had a very drawn face, possibly gaunt looking, with stubble on his chin.

He had a friendly voice, so I told him what I was doing. He then asked me was I hungry, but I said no. He went on to say that he knew where some apple trees were and I knew what he was on about as my brother and I had been there before, so I went with him. We walked towards Tranent Primary School. Across the road from the school was a brick wall and behind the wall were the apple trees. Close by there was also a small tip and as we approached, he intimated that we needed to go down a small dirt path towards the tip area where there were mounds of grass.

He took me behind the mounds so we couldn't be seen from the road. The man then asked how old I was, and I said I was about ten years old and I told him I wanted to go.

He said, "No," and grabbed my arm with his left hand and undid my trousers with the other before he put his right hand down and began to get me aroused by masturbating me.

This lasted for about five minutes before he just stopped. I then had a pee before fastening my trousers and he asked me what I was going to do now.

I said I was going home.

He asked me where home was, but I never told him where and then we started walking away with him at the side of me.

I watched him walk towards a row of houses which faced the rubbish tip and got the feeling he must have lived in one of them.

I still have nightmares about him.

.oOo.

Around March 1974, I was expelled from infant school. I punched another boy; all I remember was that he said something to me, and I knocked him out.

My behaviour was way out of control, it was around this time I ran away from Coalgate Avenue. I remember seeing men doing road works, near a place called Long Niddrie. I was really hungry, saw their works van, and took their lunch. Oops!

The next thing I knew, miles later, the police found me, in those days the police did do a good job.

They asked me where I was going.

I just said, "Down the road!"

They knew I was from the home and took me back.

Once again, I was scared. I often wonder what might have been if I had got away, that day.

I didn't get any additional punishment for running away or getting expelled. I didn't need to as the abuse was taking place all the time.

.oOo.

I have never been close to my mother, to be honest I cannot stand her. During my time at Tranent she and her new boyfriend took me out for the day – about four or five times. I remember she wanted to marry him, and they planned for a two or three week holiday to Inverness when I was about nine years old. I was meant to go with them, but Mum decided I couldn't due to my bedwetting. She didn't want it to put her new boyfriend off. So, Instead, I stayed at Tranent whilst three of my siblings went on the holiday with Mum.

Of course I was subjected to humiliation by Anna about it.

When Mum came back, she brought me a present, but I threw it away and said, "I don't want fuck all from you, get lost."

This incident made my behaviour even worse.

.oOo.

Due to be expelled, I think some of the staff thought I had psychological and behavioural problems and I was sent to a psychiatric home called Forteviot for four months. I can't remember much about it – according to social service records, I was on strong medication, at the time.

It was a big place, full of kids with perceived behavioural or psychological problems and very strict. A lot of the children were wild.

I slept in a dormitory which was always locked at night. Most of the time you weren't allowed out of your bed. Despite this, every night there would be lots of fights and, if you were caught fighting, the staff would punish you by marching you down the corridor with your arm up your back.

The only staff member I can recall at Forteviot was Nurse T who was about thirty to thirty-five years of age, and was slim with shoulder length dark, brown hair with a fair complexion. She would tie me to my bed by my hands only - to stop me getting out of bed. On some occasions she would sit on me and slap me about the face and on other occasions, she would sit on me and put her hand down my pyjamas and stroke me around my groin in order to arouse me. She just stroked me, but I don't recall her ever masturbating me. She always remained clothed.

She would also give me a bath in scolding hot water and then scrub me really hard which hurt really badly so much that I would scream my head off.

There were, obviously, other members of staff there too but no-one ever came to help me, it was that sort of place.

I also stayed in another psychiatric home called Tenterfield for around six to eight weeks, but I have no real memories of the place.

.oOo.

I got sent back to Coalgate Avenue when I was about nine or ten. I was terrified about what would happen to me when I got back there. Margaret, George and Anna were still there and a new member of staff, Rita, had also joined.

My temper and behaviour got worse. I was always fighting and getting into trouble.

Anna continued the abusive behaviour and targeted me and made my return very unpleasant. On one occasion she caught me and Alistair fighting, and she went to grab hold of me. I tried to get away and fell against the corner of the bunkbed. I split my ear open, and it was bleeding quite a bit. She called me a stupid idiot. I still have a scar on my ear to this day.

When I was about ten or eleven years of age, due to my bedwetting problem, Margaret made me put a nappy on in front of Anna and George and Margaret's two children as well as a number of the other residents.

I remember Margaret telling everyone to come and look at me having the nappy put on and I remember it being very humiliating and embarrassing.

I was crying and George shouted at me, saying, "Stop bubbling like a bairn."

They also gave me names like 'Pee the bed', 'Thicko' and 'Ugly' which made me feel totally unwanted and neglected.

Rita was another member of staff and had short, curly hair, which was dark and possibly permed. She was very over familiar with us children, particularly at night-time when she tucked you up in bed. She would hug and kiss me but it was in such a way that made me feel uncomfortable, and she would put her body against me telling me to kiss her on the lips.

Whilst she was doing this, she would be putting her hands over my legs and groin area, although it was always over the top of the bedding.

I would say she was trying to arouse me, and she appeared to get some sexual pleasure from doing this. The way it was done, it was quite clear to me that this wasn't right, and it was more than somebody just being kind and affectionate. Rita was clearly enjoying what she was doing, and it happened more than once. I'm not sure if she did this to anyone else.

.oOo.

The staff, especially Anna, used to tell me that I was nothing and I would get nowhere in life.

I had a mate who stayed at a similar family home further up the road from ours. None of what happened to me and everyone else in our home happened in his home. When I found that out, I felt lost and numb. It was the first time it occurred to me that it was only happening in our house. I was absolutely terrified to tell anyone about any of it. If that is what they did to me normally it didn't bear thinking about what they would do to me if I spoke out.

I ran away again from the home. I got as far as MacMerry before I was caught.

Larry, my social worker, continued to visit me regularly but I was still too scared to tell him anything.

My Mum sometimes visited and took Martin, Jenny and myself for days out – like going to the zoo.

I started primary school, but it did not last long; I was fighting, stealing and causing havoc with teachers. I was disciplined in a terrible way, made to stand in a corner, facing the wall, and called a dunce, just like in the home.

Once again, I was expelled. That time because I had been throwing things at the teacher.

Tranent was no easy place to grow up in. All the abuse from the staff there still gives me nightmares and affects me to this day.

It was time to move to another home.

Harmany School, Balerno

At about eleven or twelve years of age at this point, I went to Save the Children School, called the Harmany School in Balerno, Midlothian. Despite being told that me and my siblings would never be split up, I was the only one of us to go to Harmany.

My two years there were horrific. The cruelty that I both witnessed and experienced was horrible - mental, physical and sexual abuse. I thought, leaving Tranent that I was getting away from that, but it was not the case.

I was always fighting; I was, to be honest, out of control. I've not got many happy memories about that home.

Harmany School as a very big place, with a long driveway leading up to the house. As you drove down the drive there were two small cottages on the right and a field on the left, where sports would take place.

The driveway led to a small car park to the front of the house, which had a large wooden door. Inside these premises there were three floors, and my room was on the second floor, with the adults room on the third floor, which was a bit smaller than the others.

As far as I can remember, the boys' rooms were to the right and the girls to the left down a corridor. There were up to seven beds in my room which was like a small dormitory.

I can remember the following children who were resident there with me - John, Darren, Emma, Ann, Shona, John, Leslie and Maureen.

Kids came in from other homes all the time and there was always fighting to see who was the hardest.

There was one big dining room where everyone ate. The food was okay, but it was always unruly. There would be food getting thrown about all the time. Sometimes the staff would just let this happen, other times there would be punishments. It was guaranteed that there would be a fight at mealtimes.

At night it was chaos when we went to bed. Everyone would mess about, and the staff would have to come in and calm things down.

I can remember the following staff members – David, Margaret, Isobelle, Sandra, Harry, Muriel and David.

They knew which parts of the body hurt the most – on your arm, underneath your thigh and the back of your neck – and you would also get your arm twisted.

Margaret had short dark curly hair, slim to medium build and aged about thirty to thirty-five years of age. Isabelle was about five foot tall, very slim, with shoulder length blonde hair, aged between thirty to thirty-five years old and she was an attractive woman. I would say that both these women were over familiar with all of us and would often invite boys and girls up to their room, sometimes together and sometimes on their own. They would then put music on like the Beach Boys, Abba and 70's disco music and would encourage the children to dance together, in particular with people they were close to. I was told to dance slowly with Anne, a girl who I got on well with. I was told to get really close to her, hug and kiss her and to put my hands on her bottom. We were also told to dance with others as well.

The staff, Margaret and Isabelle, would also dance with me to slow music and they would hug and kiss me and rub against me in a sexual way. I remember, one night, that she asked me to put my hands on her bum.

Isabelle would rub up against me to get me aroused and then move away and point in order to embarrass me.

On one occasion as she pressed up against me and said, "He's got me right in the middle," directing her comment to Margaret.

Margaret also did the same and on one occasion in her room, she asked me did I want to see her without her top on.

I said, "No."

She was quite persistent.

I just wanted to get out of her room, and I felt very uncomfortable.

Both Margaret and Isabelle seemed to get a kick out of this, and it was as if they were having a laugh.

It should never have happened what with us being young, vulnerable and unaware. We just went along with it, thinking, at the time, it was okay.

There were two other members of staff called Sandy and Lesley who were in a relationship. Whilst they did not get involved like Margaret and Isabelle, they would watch what was going on.

.oOo.

There was another staff member there whom I can only recall as Sandra who was about thirty-five to forty years old, stocky and who wore glasses. She had brown hair, which was wavy and just short of shoulder length, with very sharp fingernails. I always called her a fat, fucking bully.

She was strong. If she caught you fighting or doing something else wrong, she would sit on you. She did this to everyone and at least a dozen times to me. When she did this, she would grab me by the genitals and dig her nails into the back of my neck which really hurt. Each time would last around twenty minutes. The pain was unimaginable.

She would also regularly pinch you which really hurt, and she would make jokes about it. It was as if this was her way of dealing with you if you were naughty and she would also twist my arm up my back.

I know there were far more incidents of physical and mental abuse, to myself, and other kids, but I cannot remember everything. Perhaps that is just as well.

If you were caught fighting, then you were taken to the "calm down room" which had soft cushions in it. You were there until you calmed down, but I could never do so. I would be throwing things about. I hated being locked in a room and, one time, I cut my hand after punching the wire window on the door.

.oOo.

When I moved to Harmany, I was in a dormitory with up to twenty others. As I got a bit older, I moved to a building called the Lower Cottage which had about sixteen children there. It was meant to help prepare the kids to get used to going to high school.

A staff member called David was in charge of the Lower Cottage. He was the worst of all the staff; over six foot tall, well built, aged between thirty-five to forty with collar length seventies style hair, which was dark black. He had a full beard and wore glasses.

He was a bully and would pick on you for nothing at all. Everybody was afraid of him, and he was very quick to slap people around.

I for one was terrified of moving to the cottage. David had already beaten me up, several times, for fighting, and I saw him, lots of times, beating other kids in the home. Once I even saw him push a child into a tree.

One night I got out of bed to go to the toilet and saw, through a gap in the door, him kissing another staff member, Margaret. I must have knocked the door as it alerted him to my being there.

He came over and shouted, "What are you doing out of bed?"

I stated I needed to go to the toilet.

I think he asked me how long I had been standing there, which I took to mean did I see him with Margaret. He then dragged me to the toilet and as he did so, he grabbed my pyjamas over my genitals and squeezed really hard, as well as slapping me all over my back and bottom. By then, I had wet myself.

He told me, "Tell anyone what you saw, you will have me to deal with."

Margaret just watched and did nothing.

.oOo.

It was during my two years here that I tried to kill myself, along with three other kids. I was about eleven years old, scared, feeling nothing and just did not want to be alive.

That day we had had simply all had enough of the abuse and bullying.

There was a poisonous bushy plant that grew outside, by the lower cottage, beside a wooden fort that the children used to play on. I remember we had been told not to touch them because they were deadly, but they were easy to pick.

So the four of us walked down to the old fort. We all took a handful of seeds and crying we looked at each other. Even though I was scared I was more scared of continuing to live. We took them at the same time. Then we waited.

What we hadn't realised is that we were seen by a member of staff - one of the few nice ones at the home – called David. He came running towards the fort and asked if we had eaten the seeds. One of the girls said 'yes,' so we were rushed to hospital.

If a member of staff had not seen us, well I would not be writing this book. It's a funny old world at times, I guess, we are meant to be in places in life for a reason.

We all went too hospital and got our stomachs pumped; it made us sick.

The next day we were back at Harmany. It was terrifying going back – not only was I scared of the staff, but high school was getting closer and my lack of education didn't help. Being expelled from the last two schools was always on my mind.

I often think back to that day and wonder about the three other kids who tried to commit suicide with me.

.oOo.

There were two teachers at Harmany who were good people - Harry and Muriel. She was a world chess champion and they were both very kind to me.

Once a week I would visit them in their house. I loved that as I could get away from Harmany, and Muriel showed me how to play chess and they would always give me an apple to eat.

There was a large field close to Harmany. In it was a big black horse with a white star on his head called Major. After being at Harry and Muriel's I would go up to this field to avoid going back into the home. Major would come up to me and say hello. Maybe he knew I was not a happy child.

I started patting and stroking him and we became friends. I would break up the apple Harry and Muriel had given me and feed it to him. On other occasions I would give him a sugar lump. Eventually I managed to get onto him and began riding him in the field without a saddle. I think I did this about seven or eight times. I remember getting bitten by a horse fly when riding Major, it bloody hurt.

Looking back at my time with Major, I feel it was like the relationship of the boy and the kestrel in the book and film *Kes*. I was certainly a lonely and skinny boy!

.oOo.

In 1977 I met the Queen and Princess Anne.

As well as being the silver jubilee in 1977, it was also the year of Save the Children, and I was one of four who were asked to carry a silver baton when it came through our area. This was probably my only happy time in this home. To be part of this was unreal.

The Queen and Princess Anne came to visit the home in 1977, I even had a Rangers hat and scarf on, when the Queen came in the classroom.

We had all been told to call her and Princess Anne, "M'am." She came into the classroom, and she went around the room speaking to some of the children.

When she got to me, she said, "Good afternoon young man, what's your name?"

I told her my name was Andrew.

"You've got the right colours on."

"Oh yeah, Rangers."

"What do you like about being here?" she asked.

I just said, "Well, your majesty, I do like the privileges," and I was being completely sarcastic.

(I did not know at the time, that I would meet the Queen and Princess Ann again years later, during my time in the army.)

.oOo.

One day, my mother came to visit me with a new pair of shoes.

"What the fuck do you want?" I said to her.

"I've just come to see you and bring you some new shoes," she replied.

I grabbed them and chucked them over a high wall and told her to, "Fuck off ya boot."

.oOo.

Around this time I started boxing. One of the staff members, David, had seen me fighting and thought I was a good boxer. I also started to do running as well – something that has helped me during life. As all runners know it's a great place to let things go, especially stress. To me it was an escape.

I did well as a runner and would get to go, with school, to places to competitively run. We won a big competition called the Scottish Thistle and went up to Rannoch in the Highlands to collect our awards.

I also remember going to celebrate the summer solstice when we were taken to the top of the Black Hill in the Pentlands and watched the sun coming up.

We were also taken to Dublin to watch Scotland take on Ireland in the Five Nations.

.oOo.

School at Harmany was chaotic, I didn't learn anything there. The classrooms had about forty children in them.

We didn't celebrate birthdays at Harmany, I think because there were too many kids there. It made me feel unwanted and rejected. My social worker, Larry, did always visit on my birthday though. Larry was ok, but I think now, how much did he really know about all of us?

I do remember going to Cinderella at Christmas as a group. Les Dawson and Rikki Fulton were in the pantomime and we met them after the show, as they knew we were from a home, and they gave us presents.

.oOo.

After two years at Harmany I moved back to Tranent to prepare me for high school. My bed wetting was still bad, but unlike at Tranent, the staff at Harmany just told you to put the bedding in the wash and get a shower.

I wonder how many children who stayed at Harmany have come forward to the inquiry, as I have been told there is a lot. Some people's statements will be public when the hearing opens for Harmany. I will not be taking part due to my mental health though. Instead, my statement is this book.

Overall, I have mixed emotions about the place as some of the staff there were really genuine and friendly but most of the others were bullies. There was an element of intimidation and fear all the time and there was always the feeling of being encouraged to be very touchy feely with other children which seemed natural at the time but looking back, was clearly very inappropriate. We didn't know any better.

In general I just tried to avoid going near any of the abusive staff there and at Tranent.

Back to Tranent

So after two years in Harmany I was sent back to the family group home in Tranent.

The same staff were still in charge however, it seemed, because I was older, they wanted to make things harder, as if they weren't already. George was still a bully, things carried on the same way with Margaret and Anna was even worse than before. It was a nightmare but ten times worse. I hated going back there.

What's more was that my sister, Wendy, and brother, Martin, had been adopted. So I had lost my siblings as well. Although I met Wendy about thirty-eight years later, I have never seen Martin since.

I started a job delivering milk when I was about thirteen and got a paper round, just to escape the abuse. I delivered the papers every day to get away from the staff at Trane–t - including on Sundays. I started the day at 5am and found this very tiring. From these jobs I got money and I was able to go to Ibrox to see Rangers play.

I also played rugby, joined army cadets, and did other activities, just to escape the family group home.

To be honest I was not ready for high school due to my lack of education and I had to go down a year. Being expelled from infant and primary school did not help. A lost childhood indeed.

The school was called Ross High School and, almost every day, for the first few years, I got the belt, along with a few other school pals for poor discipline. I did not know any different. I came from a care home, not a family, and I felt different to other kids who had parents to go home to.

There was homework to do every night and I began to play rugby and started to box again.

The teachers would each carry a belt around with them and they would strike your hand. On one occasion, my friend Kenny stole my pencil and, as I did not have it in class, I got the belt. Still, I didn't snitch on Kenny.

As well as Kenny, I made some good friends in school, especially Jim, Craig, Scott and the twins Graham & Stuart. They all had mums and dads and I would often go back to their homes after school or at the weekend to get away from Tranent.

It really helped having a few friends, during my horrible childhood, so I can't thank them enough. It was hard to hide what was going on as I was always very scared. Thanks also to jill, the twin's sister, who is a lovely friend still today. Kenny's parents were always good to me. His Dad would often say, "Looking a bit skinny son, you want a butty?"

As if I would say no.

Another thing he would say to me was, "Here's the laddie from the home, better get him some food."

The food at Tranent was poor and I really was skinny.

.oOo.

Back at the house, there was a TV in the living room. Anna and Margaret would make me watch really scary films like *The Exorcist* and some of the Hammer Films like *Curse of the Werewolf* and laugh at me. The abuse and humiliation just carried on. One night, I could not sleep, as I was so scared of a film I had watched.

I also went to Sunday school, yet again to escape the home.

I did have bumps and bruises on my body, as a result of being hit, but was always too terrified to say anything. I was always scared to change in front of other kids, because of –his - at the home and in school.

.oOo.

I joined the Royal Scots Regiment army cadets, to escape being in Tranent. I loved being in the cadets and I would go every Tuesday and Thursday each week and we would also go away for camps at the weekends twice a month which were great. I learnt a lot of skills and, even though I struggled due to my lack of education, I was awarded four stars for learning about first aid, map reading and shooting.

Being in the cadets gave me the drive and determination to join the army.

I wanted to join the army, as I did a few years later, once again to escape my horrible childhood.

.oOo.

One time in school, I found a maths books with the answers in the back. During a lesson, I just copied the answers down but my teacher, Mrs S, queried how I could have got everything right when, usually, I didn't. I just started laughing and told her the answers were in the back of the book.

"Right," she shouted, "front of the class now for the belt," but every time she tried to belt me, I moved my hands away and laughed.

"Mr Johnson's office now, you'll get the belt off him," she ordered.

Mr Johnson was the hardest at giving the belt at school and he gave me four of the best and I cried.

.oOo.

Thanks to the army cadets and my paper round, I could escape from the home. I was getting older and my time at high school was getting close to an end, this worried me due to lack of education.

I left school without any good grades at all, no wonder, but I had to get out of Tranent, so it was joining the army or nothing. Where I lived, if you didn't have a good education, or money, then you had no chance of getting a job. No-one at the home had any interest in what I – and the others – were going to do. Basically, once you were eighteen you were out of the care system and not their responsibility anymore.

I went for my entrance test but due to my lack of education, I failed it. Returning to Tranent, I was the subject to humiliation from the staff, especially Anna.

All was not lost, as I found out about night school and studied English and Maths and after lots of hard work for months, I then tried again for the Army.

This time I passed with 98 percent, I thought to myself, all to all those horrible bastards, you can all fuck right off.

.oOo.

As it got to the last few days of my time there, I started to get stuff together. I had kept a rare collection of Marvel comics, but they had gone missing. Anna had binned them saying I would not need them, and I told her to fuck off, called her a cow and stuck two fingers up too her, and continued, "Thank fuck I won't see you again."

I always think back if I had not got in the army, where my life would have gone? I am pretty certain that joining the army saved my life.

I left Tranent in 1981, to join junior service in the army, which was for those aged sixteen to eighteen, it was very hard, but I soon settled down.

The Army

I joined the regular army in 1982, the Royal Scots. I left the Army seven years later in January 1989 so I could spend time with my eldest daughter, Laura, and see her grow up. I could not settle in civi life though, so I joined the Territorial Army after a few years, in 1993.

Joining the army gave me a sense of purpose in life and an escape route from my past.

I had already learnt first aid whilst in the cadets and during training I also was taught map reading, weapon drill and field craft (such as how to use camouflage) amongst other things.

.oOo.

Somehow Mum found out I got in the army and started to contact me. Having nowhere to go on leave, I had to go to hers in Leicester, which I hated. As soon as I was there she asked me for money, for 'keep' even though I had never even stayed with her from the time I went into the care system.

Most of the time I went out to get away from her, so even after my hell in the homes, I had to put up with a mum

I did not even like. At first I didn't really think about her asking for money, but when she started asking for more and more, almost every other day, we ended up rowing. Finally I told her to piss off, packed a few things and went to stay with a girl I had met on leave.

My second leave I could not even go to hers, as she was having problems, I had to stay in the army camp. The army was now all I had.

At the start of my book there is a conversation between Mum and myself. Here, you will find some proper context to that conversation.

It was 1981, I was just to pass out as a junior soldier in the Royal Scots and be presented with two awards. My mum had said she would be there.

It was a grey, cloudy day at the Bridge of Don barracks in Aberdeen and I was getting my dress uniform on - Glengarry, brogues and my tartan trews dress tunic. My passing out parade was one of the biggest days of my life.

Suddenly, I was called to the Sergeant Major's office, and I knocked on his office door.

"Is that you young McDowell?" he asked.

"Yes sir," I replied.

"Come in son."

My first thought was why did Boss Hogg just call me son? We called him Boss Hogg as he was short and stocky just like the character from the Dukes of Hazzard on TV.

I was told to sit down as he opened an old filing cabinet drawer, took out a bottle of whisky with two glasses and poured us both a drink. He said, "Cheers son," and told me

I had done well in my training, considering where I'd come from.

I said, "Many thanks, Sir."

He said, "Call me Dave. You're a trained soldier now." Then he added, "I just had a call from your mother, she can't make it today."

I felt empty inside. Once again, my so called mother let me down. It was my passing out parade and I had no-one there. This still affects me today.

Dave clearly knew how much it would hurt me and said, "You are welcome to stay with me on leave."

I said thanks again and we chatted about training and what I wanted to do. He said he knew I had a friend in training, Ricky, and told me to see if I could also stay with him. I went back to my barrack room, saw everyone's families walking round, which hurt again, as it reminded me that I had no-one.

The passing out parade itself was very surreal. I felt like the only person on parade that day as everyone else had family there. It was an empty feeling. I felt alone, and it still bothers me to this day to be honest. It also taught me one thing, never let your own kids down.

Later, I spoke to Ricky, told him what had happened, met his parents and they said come and stay with us. I let the sergeant major know and my travel warrant was changed.

I stayed in Glasgow with Ricky and had some good RNR – rest and recreation – which basically meant we went out on the piss. Two days into leave, Ricky said I better call my mum so I did.

"Where are you?" She barked down the phone.

"I'm in Glasgow," I reply.

"Aren't you coming home for leave?"

"No, I'm not."

"Why not? This is your home."

"No, it's not my home and you're not my mother," and I slammed down the phone.

Once my leave had finished, I proceeded to my regiment.

The Falklands War was taking place just as I was about to pass out and I was worried about being called up to go and fight but luckily it finished in June of 1982.

Throughout my time in the army I had no-one to call or write to. Everyone else had family to ring or write to. I always remember when the post arrived and was given out to everyone else apart from me. It made me feel as if I was on my own.

.oOo.

In 1984 my regiment went to the Falklands. There was still a lot of work to be done there after the war two years earlier such as building portacabins, finding mines and generally cleaning up. We were still finding weapons from the war.

It was an amazing place to visit. I saw sharks and, when we sent to South Georgia, we were chased by elephant seals.

.oOo.

For about five years of my time in the army I was stationed in Germany as part of the British Army on the Rhine (BAOR) and was taught how to drive a mechanised armour vehicle.

I never went back to the UK during that whole time.

All I wanted to do in the Army was to get my crossed swords which meant I would be a Physical Training Instructor (PTI). You had to be at the top of your game to do the course. Most of the instructors were in the PT core. It was always my aim, but was never an elite at any sport, which is why they are such brilliant instructors. Although it was tough, I was proud to be nominated top student in my section.

While on my PTI course, I was very fit and on one of the 8 mile course runs, when I found myself running with one of the instructors who was an international fell runner. While we were running, he said, "Look behind you!"

I did, and the rest of the course were nowhere to be seen.

He said, "They are about 2 mins behind." He was not even out of breath. Then he added, "If you want to get in the PT Core, you need to be a different level of fitness."

I thought, 'What does he mean?'

He then said, "We have about 3 quarters of a mile to go, try and stay with me," then whoosh he shot off like a rocket.

No chance I was keeping up, and I thought I was fit.

At the finish, he said, "Well done, but now you know the level you need to be for the core."

Just goes to show, that is why we are the best Army in the world. The PT Core has always had the cream of top athletes in it. I was just glad, to pass the course.

We had to learn all about anatomy and physiology and how to prepare lesson plans as well as having to pass hard physical fitness tests ourselves.

My instructor was a hockey player who went on to play for Great Britain in the 1988 Olympics in Seoul, South Korea.

Eighty people joined the course and only thirty-two passed it, including me, and I was able to teach recruits on getting into shape.

As a PTI, I was able to work on the Kypton Factor Assault Course.

I well remember standing on the six-foot wall of the Krypton Factor assault course one beautiful warm day thinking, 'Wow, I've done it." One of my ambitions in life had been achieved by being a PTI. I thought back to those who said I would never get anywhere in life. Well I said to myself, here I am!

It was a fantastic time in my Army career, something I will always remember.

The was one night we were on night patrol exercise, yours truly had a night flare, as a section commander. I set it of, but it seemed to have not worked.

My mate said, "Well that never worked!"

We both laughed, next thing, we saw flames, then more and more.

Lads started coming out of bushes and tress. The whole area was on fire. Then we heard on radio the fire brigade was called and it was eventually put out.

My mate never said a thing. What a night that was.

When it came to leave the army, I toured Europe visiting countries such as France, the Netherlands and Italy. I also travelled to watch Rangers play in the UEFA Cup.

.oOo.

After the Army

I married when I was in the army and we had a daughter, Laura, who was born in Germany. When I left the army, I moved to Warrington to be close to my oldest daughter Laura and try and make a go of my marriage - but it didn't work out. I was too young and immature and so eventually we divorced. I met another woman, we had our daughter, Cloe, and moved to Northwest England. Sadly, that did not work out either.

Both mums are fantastic parents to their daughters and I'm still friends with them. I still get on well with Laura's mum and family. They are all lovely.

I remember when Cloe was born that I wrote and sent photographs of her to my Mum. The letter was returned, in her handwriting, saying not known at this address.

I liked becoming a father - it was exciting and did give me a feeling of a family. I suppose due to my childhood there has always been this feeling of being detached and alone. Long lasting effects of childhood abuse in my life. However, what keep me going now are my two beautiful girls. I will always be there for them, as they are only kids a short time. Being a parent never stops – even when they become adults. I just want them to live a full and happy life. Who knows, maybe I will find that special lady one day.

I never had many relationships afterwards and went from job to job including working in a steel factory.

.oOo.

During that time I became team manager of Warrington Athletics Club we qualified for the National Round Relay Championships which was an amazing achievement for a non-league team.

We took sixteen runners to the event which was in Wigan, and I was on the starting line with famous runners including Dave Moorcroft and Rob Denmark.

After the race, I met up with Sebastian Coe (now Lord Coe). He was a really nice guy who had time for everyone but as we were leaving I called over to him, "Vote Labour."

Everyone laughed and it's still a joke at the club.

.oOo.

I did look at a civil claim for compensation regarding the abuse I suffered whilst in all the care homes. All was fine at first, they found over 100 pages of records, witness statements, and my enquiry statement - but then the redress scheme came along, and everything changed.

This all happened over lockdown. The Scottish government decided that no-one could bring a civil claim for compensation, instead everyone had to apply to this so-called redress scheme. None of us asked for this scheme. Having to apply to it is a massive insult to us survivors. To me, the government have not thought about us at all, rather, it is there to make it look like they have done something to help.

To me it is all corrupt to the core. The redress scheme offers payments to survivors, but you can't if you try to do anything else about proper redress which to me isn't just about compensation but justice.

I have had three different solicitors look at my case, but in the end they all said the same fucking crap, 'Not enough evidence, your best option is the redress scheme.'

We will never get a fair trial in all this. A lot of survivors want not just redress but justice and therefore I'm so unhappy with the Scottish Government. In my view, is a massive cover up.

.oOo.

Wendy is my youngest sister. In 2015, I met up with her after thirty-eight years apart. Things were okay to start with, but with all the years apart, and the hurt in our lives, it has been very difficult to really know each other.

I also found out I had three other siblings through Birth Link. They were the children of my Dad who had remarried after leaving Mum. They had not been in care and their childhood had been all right.

I found them myself through Facebook. If I had waited for Birth Link to have found them, it would have taken ages.

Then, with my Cloe, we met one of them, Caroline, in 2022. It felt the same situation as with Wendy. I was worried about this, but it has been good, we are slowly building a family bond, but it has been affected by all that has been taken away, due to the failed care system in Scotland. Caroline and I are fine, but it has been a slow process. It's been really difficult with Wendy due to everything that has gone on.

This is all down to the failed care system in Scotland in the 1970s. I still don't know my real family. No matter what, I love them all.

Life after the army, well it has never been easy, failed relationships, and in and out of jobs. I did join the reserves – which I loved – and did really well in it. I joined, firstly, with the Kings Regiment and then the Royal Engineers.

It has really only been the last four years from 2018 until 2022, that life is better. I still have a battle with childhood trauma and PTSD and I'm now having treatment, which is very hard. There is a long way to go. I don't know what has given me inner strength to carry on, but suppose you have to fight back somehow. As a survivor all I want is justice, and the truth to be known.

Life nowadays, maybe a little better, I have had the first phase of treatment for PTSD and childhood trauma, with the second phase later in the year. Which will be the hardest part. My two daughters, make me proud everyday, they mean the world to me. It was a pleasure watching them grow and become who they are today. Laura is such an amazing person, who has to overcome the challenges of

Autism and Aspergers Syndrome, her courage is just amazing. So proud of her.

My younger daughter Cloe, wow, just so proud that she is now at university. The day I took her was one of my proudest of my life.

Please don't sit in silence if you have had any abuse ever, speak up and fight back. I still don't know were I got the strength to fight back to this day, maybe something inside me always made me carry on. So my message is, never give up, no mater what.

Breaking the Ice

The abuse I received at home and in care still affects me today. It has caused issues with relationships and trusting people.

When I was a child, for a long time I thought the abuse was normal. I was always terrified and looking over my shoulder. As an adult, I started getting flashbacks, especially when my daughters were getting older. I think when they were little, I had to focus on them far more but as they got older I had more time to think. That's when it really hit me.

I had terrible nightmares, about my time in the army, and my horrible childhood. In my dreams I could see my abusers, pointing at me and laughing. They would humiliate me. Make me feel ashamed. That is a lot of what the abuse was like.

It is like I had no anchor and no ties to family to keep me grounded. I still felt alone and isolated. Even when invited to a party by close friends, I always (or most of the time) just felt cut off and detached.

In around 2007 I was sleeping rough for about four months and then kipping at a friend's house. Then the

Royal British Legion helped me find a house through their benevolent fund and it helped me get back on my feet.

One day, in 2017, I was just chatting to Mandy in the Legion and I told her that I got flashbacks about the army and school. She told me I must have PTSD and kindly helped organise the initial appointment with a clinical psychologist at Veterans In Mind.

I was sent up to Edinburgh before lockdown to see a top clinical psychologist, by the Scottish Child Abuse Inquiry. I was told that all survivors that came to the inquiry have done this. The initial report from the psychologist was delayed due to lockdown in 2020. When it did come through the conclusion was that I suffer from complex Post Traumatic Stress Disorder (PTSD) and that I needed trauma focused psychotherapy intervention.

The psychologist talked to me about my life and saw that, apart from my strong relationship with my daughters, there was nothing motivating me to stay alive. Without Cloe and Laura I was upset, felt down and struggled with life. The thing was the girls were getting older and wanted to spend time with her friends. Of course, I was happy for them – I am the best Dad in the world to my daughters – but I was personally worried about the long-term impact of increasing social isolation would have on me.

The first phase of treatment has helped though, a lot. The next phase will be the hardest, but I will not give up. The childhood I had will never leave me, but it won't beat me. Writing my story in this book has also helped me put it all in context.

.oOo.

As part of the Royal British Legion's 100 years Anniversary I also got nominated for a recognition award. I went to London in 2021, it was fantastic, at Westminster Abbey, with the late Queen, and Princess Anne, in attendance. It was a day I will never forget.

The reason I was invited was because I took over as a Poppy Appeal organiser where I now live. I started going into schools and making more people aware of the Legion and what it does.

The Legion wanted ideas for their centenary, and I thought up the idea of going into local schools and running a Remembrance Day themed arts competition. Ten schools took part and the children's work was displayed in the local shopping centre. We started this in 2021 and repeated it for 2022 as part of the Jubilee celebrations as well.

I never thought from the Silver Jubilee in 1977, that I would have had anything to do with late Queens Diamond Jubilee, so many years later.

It was a huge success and we raised thousands of pounds for the Legion. It felt so good to help the Legion because of the help they gave me when I was homeless – and it feels like I am giving something back.

.oOo.

Another thing that has always been there is music. It helps me cope and has been an escape, especially Ska and Mod music such as Madness, the Specials, the Jam and the Beat. I even met Suggs from Madness on his solo tour, about his life. We talked about our lives, and I found out he had a sister he never knew of before, just like me.

Meeting Suggs was amazing, it is not every day you meet one of your idols. Suggs signed his book for me, for myself and my sister Wendy.

He said, "It's funny in life, that we can all share similar stories."

Recently, I've been following a new Ska band, the brilliant Death of Guitar Pop. As a fan I was proud to help crowdfund their third album and even have my name on the album sleeve. In 2022 and 2023 I got to meet the two main men; Silky and Top Kat at their sound check and they and their music have really helped me especially on the bad days.

I made a point to tell them how much their music has supported my mental health. All three of their albums are just fantastic. They are also a band that really gives a lot of time for the fans. They also support MIND, a mental health charity – the same charity that I plan to donate the proceeds from this book too. I am so grateful to Silky and Top Kat and I love being part of the DOP family – Ska forever!

.oOo.

Certain things do still hurt me. One is growing up and not really knowing my real dad, another being unable to celebrate important birthdays with my siblings throughout my life. I upsets me that I don't really know my niblings (ie my nieces and nephews) either.

I have always hated Mother's Day. So many people I know had a real and loving mother, and to them it is a day when they celebrate the love and support their mother gave them. To me it is just a reminder that mine was a bastard. Don't get me wrong though, I don't begrudge my friends being able to enjoy those occasions, but to me it is just something that reminds me of all the hurt I had to endure, and often makes me feel very alone.

.oOo.

Where I now live, I became friends with a lovely man, named Mr Webster, through doing his garden. A bond was formed, and he became like a father to me. He was an old school gent, a legend.

Cloe and I would go and watch him compete in many speech and drama competitions such as the Liverpool Arts Festival. He won many awards and was well known in the competition circle. We would celebrate many events together such as Burns Night, St George's Day and St Andrew's Day.

Finally I felt that I had found that connection that my friends seem to have growing up, and a parent figure in Mr Webster. He was someone who cared about me and Cloe and someone that I felt I could turn to in need.

In 2008 he asked for my date of birth and some other details and said something about his house. I told him that I did not want anything from him as I valued his friendship. Mr Websiter sadly passed away in 2015 and left his house in his will for me and Cloe – his generosity will be remembered my whole life, but the connection and company he gave me is valued even more.

We live in his house now. It just goes to show what kindness can bring in life and even a childhood frozen in time and thaw a little.

.oOo.

And with that thought, I remember the song by Richard Ashcroft, 'This Thing Called Life'. I paraphrase the lyrics and what they mean to me.

Let us dare to try, to persevere, no matter the odds that stand before us. We must learn to navigate against the tide, to shed the weight and embrace the humbling lessons that life has to offer.

Past misdeeds hold no true power over us; they are just dust in the winds of time. We must unlock the chains that bind us - others may have inflicted wounds on us, but it does not define our worth. We must learn that the allure of temporary escape, such as drugs, only serves to mask the pain unless we confront the true sources of our suffering.

We can break free from the shackles that hold us back, and with each step forward, we embark on a journey of healing and self-discovery.

Printed in Great Britain
by Amazon